NOW YOU CAN READ.....
JESUS THE SHEPHERD

STORY RETOLD BY LEONARD MATTHEWS

ILLUSTRATED BY CLIVE UPTTON

Library of Congress Cataloging in Publication Data

Matthews, Leonard.
   Jesus the shepherd.

   (Now you can read Bible stories)
   Summary: Retells two parables, "The Lost Sheep" and "The Prodigal Son", that Jesus Christ told to His followers.
   1. Jesus Christ—Person and offices—Juvenile literature.   2. Lost sheep (Parable)—Juvenile literature.   3. Prodigal son (Parable)—Juvenile literature.   4. Bible.   N.T.   John X, 1-18—Paraphrases, English.   5. Shepherds in the Bible—Juvenile literature.   6. Bible stories, English—N.T. Gospels.   [1. Bible stories—N.T.   2. Parables]
I. Title.   II. Series: Now you can read—Bible stories.
BT205.M377   1984   226'.809505   84-15902
ISBN 0-86625-302-5

Published by Rourke Publications, Inc., P.O. Box 3328, Vero Beach, Florida 32964. Copyright © 1984 by Rourke Publications, Inc. All copyrights reserved. No part of this book may be reproduced in any form without written permission from the publisher. Printed in the United States of America.
   The Publishers acknowledge permission from Brimax Books for the use of the name "Now You Can Read" and "Large Type For First Readers" which identify Brimax Now You Can Read series.

GROLIER ENTERPRISES CORP.

NOW YOU CAN READ.....
JESUS THE SHEPHERD

Jesus was becoming well known. Crowds followed Him everywhere. They wanted to hear Him speak. He spoke to everyone, rich or poor.

He spoke to beggars. He also made friends with Roman soldiers. This made Him many enemies.

The Romans had conquered Israel. Their rule was strict. The people hated them.

The priests were among those who
hated Jesus. They did not believe
He was the Son of God. They did
not understand why He spoke to
Romans, beggars and thieves.
Jesus knew this, so one day He
told them why.

"Most people," He said, "believe in God. This makes God very happy. There are many people, though, who do not believe in God." This made the priests very angry.

"Nobody should have anything to do with those people," shouted the priests. "They should be punished."

Jesus shook His head. "No," He said. "We should talk to these people. We should try to make friends with them. We should do all we can to make them believe in God and love Him. God is always hoping that one day those who do not believe in Him will do so."

"To God, a man who does not believe in Him is like a child who has lost his way. How happy we all are when a lost child is found again. At such a time he means more to us than the children who have not been lost." The priests did not wish to hear more.

The priests went away. Jesus smiled at the people who had stayed to listen. He could see that many of them had not really understood what He had said.

They were simple people. Jesus decided to tell them a story.

"First," Jesus began, "you must understand that to God we are all like sheep. God is our shepherd. We are His flock."

Then Jesus said, "He takes care of us just as a shepherd takes care of his sheep."

This is the story
that Jesus told
the people.
At the end of each
day the shepherd
counted the sheep
in his flock.

There were one hundred sheep in
the flock. One day one was missing.

What could have happened to the missing sheep? It must have wandered away during the day. It would have to be found. The shepherd asked a friend to look after his flock. Then he set out to find the lost sheep.

Did one sheep out of a hundred really matter all that much? To the shepherd it meant *very* much. The ninety-nine sheep were safe in their meadow. The lost sheep might be in danger. There were always wolves waiting to attack sheep. The shepherd was very worried.

It was important that the lost sheep be found as soon as possible. The shepherd made his way back to the field where the sheep had been all day. There was no sign of it. He called out to the sheep.

All his sheep knew his voice.

The missing sheep did not come running toward him. He set off to look for the sheep. He walked for miles across the rocky desert.

It was not safe for a man to be
alone in the desert. That was
where many wild animals roamed.
Hungry wolves would attack a man
just as quickly as they would
attack a sheep.

Bravely the shepherd went on searching. Night had fallen by the time he found his missing sheep. Luckily, it was not hurt. It was just tired and shivering from the cold.

The shepherd was tired, too. However, he picked up the heavy animal. He carried it on his shoulders and set off for home.

All through the night he carried
the sheep. He arrived back safely.
He was so happy! His friends
welcomed him back. "See! I have
found my missing sheep," the
shepherd called out.

Then the shepherd decided to hold a feast. "Let us share our joy," he said. "My lost sheep is found again." Everyone agreed.

As Jesus ended His story, He smiled at the people listening to Him. "The shepherd was happy because he had found his sheep," He said.

Then Jesus explained, "So God, our Shepherd, is happy when someone who has been lost to Him, starts to believe in Him."

Now the people understood why gentle Jesus spoke to everyone, no matter who that person was.

All these appear in the pages of the story. Can you find them?

Jesus

shepherd's friend

wolf

beggar

shepherd

lost sheep

Now tell the story in your own words.